Key Stage 2
English
Spelling & Vocabulary

WORKBOOK 7

Intermediate Level

Dr Stephen C Curran

with Warren Vokes

Edited by Mark Schofield

This book belongs to

Accelerated Education Publications Ltd

discover ✗	distinct	discuss
distress	size	prize
dislike ✓	disgrace	nation ✗
station	dictation	motion

Exercise 139a

1) He scored a bull's-eye with the very last __bullet__ that he fired.

2) The draymen unloaded the first __barrel__ of beer and lowered it into the cellar.

3) A secretary should be qualified in both shorthand and __dictation__ .

4) The ship was in __motion__ and in danger of sinking.

5) Houdini was an expert escapologist whose acts would __astonish__ his audiences.

6) A __bullet__ fired from a crossbow mortally wounded Richard the Lion-heart.

7) His bicycle tyre was old and the __rubber__ had perished.

8) "There is a __quarrel__ possibility that the match will be cancelled."

9) He sold some __company__ shares to raise more capital.

10) His __rubber__ bull fetched the highest price at the market.

Score [/10]

Exercise 139b

11) Her behaviour was a __disgrace__ and her friends were embarrassed.

12) Sancho Panza was Don Quixote's __companion__ and shared his adventures.

13) The rebel troops commandeered the airport and the television __station__ .

14) His waistline had increased and his trousers needed to be a __size__ larger.

15) They used the personal column to __publish__ the news of their baby's birth.

16) In years to come we may __discover__ that life does exist on other planets.

17) "We need to sit down together and __disscus__ the problems that we face."

18) The rolling __motion__ of the ship in the rough weather made her feel seasick.

19) "We may __dislike__ many laws but it is our duty to obey them."

20) Britain is said to be a __nation__ of animal lovers.

Score [/10]

Across

(139)

3. Clearly different and separate.
5. A large cylindrical cask used to store liquids.
11. A test or exercise of language comprehension in which pupils write down words spoken aloud by a teacher.
12. A stop on a railway route.
13. Being together with others.
17. To prepare and produce material in printed or electronic form.
18. Ammunition used in a firearm.
19. To consider something or somebody disagreeable or unpleasant.
20. An angry dispute between people.

Down

1. To find out information that was not previously known.
2. The amount, scope, or degree of something, in terms of how large or small it is.
4. Somebody to be with.
6. The act or process of moving.
7. The people who live in a land under a single government.
8. Mental suffering or physical hardship or difficulty.
9. To talk about a subject with others.
10. Shame or loss of respect arising from bad behaviour.
14. Amaze somebody greatly.
15. A naturally occurring elastic substance.
16. An award for the winner of a contest or competition.

Put the mystery letter (✳) into the box marked **139** below. Add in the mystery letters from puzzles **140** to **146** then rearrange them to make **Oliver's Mystery Word**. The clue is **FURNITURE**.

139	140	141	142	143	144	145	146

Now rearrange them:

Mystery Word:

Score /20

3

question   **appear**   **quart**
quarter   **horrid**   **coffee**
occur   **occupy**   **belief**
believe   **grieve**   **ourselves**

Across

2. A part detached from the whole.
5. To live in a place.
7. Plural of 'wharf'.
9. The daughter of a sibling.
11. One of four parts.
13. Past participle of 'occupy'.
17. Not remembered.
19. To experience intense sorrow.
20. A landing place for ships.

140

Down

1. To accept that something is true or real.
3. Strong, caffeine-rich drink.
4. To happen or come about.
6. A written or spoken inquiry.
8. Dreadful, shocking, or frightening enough to cause horror.
10. An opinion, especially a firm and considered one.
12. Two pints or a quarter of a gallon.
14. To join or mix together.
15. Refers emphatically to us.
16. Not solid and having empty space inside.
18. To come into view.

Mystery Letter [ ]

Score [/ 20]

4

wharf	wharves	
niece	piece	**Word Bank**
occupied	hollow	**TOTAL**
forgotten	combine	**2,800**

Exercise 140a

1) It was a _question_ of honour and he accepted the challenge.

2) More women now _combine_ having a career and being a mother.

3) A _belif_ in existentialism requires a person to shape their own destiny.

4) He checked all the components and found that one _piece_ was missing.

5) It was a long time since she last knitted and she had _forgoten_ how to cast on.

6) "Didn't it _occur_ to you that you might hurt her feelings?"

7) A gallon of milk was divided equally and poured into four one- _quard_ containers.

8) The Channel Islands were _occupied_ by German troops during World War II.

9) The ships had departed and all the _wharves_ were empty.

10) He ground the _coffee_ beans ready for the percolator.   **Score** | 10 |

Exercise 140b

11) It seemed impossible: she could not _belive_ that she had passed the exam.

12) His apology sounded _hollow_ and insincere.

13) The children continued to _grieve_ for many months after the death of their aunt.

14) "Hurry up! It's almost a _quater_ to, and the game kicks off at three o'clock."

15) Many of us have doubts and fears that are difficult to admit even to _ourselves_.

16) The mixture smelled disgusting and left a _horrid_ taste in her mouth.

17) The events of that tragic night _occupy_ my thoughts as I recount the details.

18) The cyclist seemed to _apped_ from nowhere and she had to swerve to avoid him.

19) The tall cranes along the _whaf_ were loading cargo into the ships.

20) His sister gave birth and he now had a new baby _nece niece_.   **Score** | 10 |

5

Exercise 141a

1) She checked her son, asleep in the bed, but he had not _Shirred_.

2) They decided to _Skirt_ around the edge of the wood.

3) The show was popular and there was a long queue at the ticket _office_.

4) She bought a _knitting_ pattern to make a jumper for her grandson.

5) The cottage cheese contained olives and sun-dried _tomatoes_.

6) She was _taught_ to swim at a very early age.

7) He lifted the _bonnet_ to check the levels of oil and water in the engine.

8) Their movements were synchronised and each dancer seemed to _mirror_ the other.

9) The guitarist played with great _skill_ and dexterity.

10) The eldest _daughter_ inherited her mother's jewellery.

Score [/ 10]

Exercise 141b

11) Roast _Potatoes_ and Yorkshire pudding are traditionally served with roast beef.

12) Their defence was _caught_ napping and the opposition scored an easy goal.

13) He moved his queen's _knight_ two squares forward and one to the right.

14) "Would it be very _naughty_ of me to have another chocolate?"

15) The 'Potato' was brought to England from South America in the sixteenth century.

16) She liked to _knit_ cardigans and bonnets for her baby granddaughter to wear.

17) Elgar's _Nimrod_, from _Enigma Variations_, never failed to _stir_ his emotions.

18) "Pass the _tomato_ ketchup, please."

19) Her first attempt failed, so she tried a _different_ approach.

20) The ship's captain gave the order to the petty _officer_.

Score [/ 10]

Across

141

1. Round vegetable with a bright red skin and pulpy, seedy flesh.
3. A garment that hangs from the waist and does not divide into two separate legs.
5. To interlock wool loops, using long needles or a machine, to make a garment.
6. Ability to do something well.
8. Roused somebody into action.
12. A glass for reflecting an image.
14. Badly behaved, being mischievous or disobedient.
16. Rounded white tubers with a thin skin cooked as a vegetable.
17. Gave lessons.
19. Unlike anything or anyone else.

Down

2. A room used for business activity.
4. Something being knitted.
7. To move a spoon, stick, or some other implement through liquid in order to mix or cool the contents.
9. Somebody's female child.
10. Past tense of 'catch'.
11. A hat framing the face and usually tied under the chin, worn by a girl or woman.
13. Medieval soldier of high rank.
15. Red vegetables that grow on climbing plants and widely eaten cooked or raw.
16. A rounded white root vegetable that can be boiled, baked, roasted or fried.
18. Someone of rank in the armed forces.

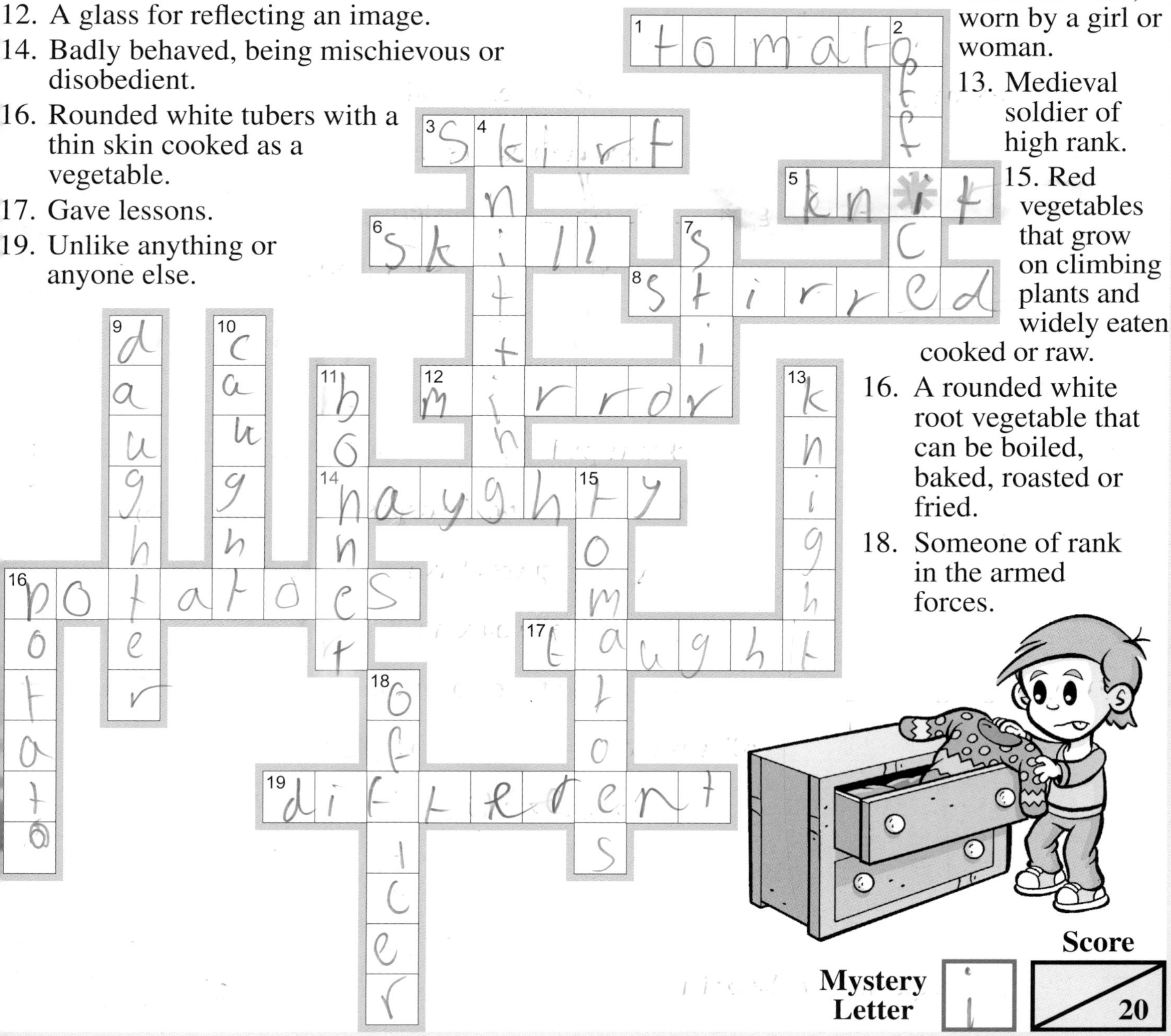

Crossword grid with answers filled in:

1 Across: tomato
3 Across: skirt
5 Across: knit
6 Across: skill
8 Across: stirred
12 Across: mirror
14 Across: naughty
16 Across: potatoes
17 Across: taught
19 Across: different

2 Down: office
4 Down: knitting
7 Down: stir
9 Down: daughter
10 Down: caught
11 Down: bonnet
13 Down: knight
15 Down: tomatoes
16 Down: potato
18 Down: officer

Score /20

Mystery Letter i

value	continue	statue
thread	instead	steadily
weary	wearily	foe
poetry	butcher	shilling

Across

142

1. Bringing a feeling of pleasure, enjoyment or satisfaction.
2. Literature work written in verse.
3. Coming in a regular nonstop flow.
8. To believe or imagine something to be the case.
9. Enemy or opponent.
10. A three-dimensional image of a human being or animal.
11. Full of, covered in, or dirtied by mud.
12. Former British coin that was equivalent to one-twentieth of a pound.
15. Adverb of 'weary'.
16. Worth, importance or usefulness of something.
17. A passageway under or through an obstruction.
18. A fine cord made of two or more twisted fibres.

Down

1. A feeling of happiness, delight or satisfaction.
4. In place of something.
5. To keep going.
6. Tired, especially having run out of strength, patience or endurance.
7. To regard something or somebody as valuable.
11. To find out the size, length, quantity, or rate of something using a suitable instrument or device.
13. Somebody who cuts up, prepares and sells meat.
14. Crafty and deceitful.

Mystery Letter

Score

20

8

© 2006 Stephen Curran

Exercise 142a

1) He used all his guile and wit to devise a _____ plan to trick his opponent.

2) _____ *Island* and *Kidnapped* were written by Robert Louis Stevenson.

3) He lost his footing on the _____ river bank, slipped and fell into the water.

4) New recruits used to be given the king's _____ when they enlisted in the army.

5) "If you _____ to disrupt the lesson, I shall send you out of the classroom!"

6) The snow fell _____ all day and covered the ground with a white carpet.

7) "It's a _____ to meet you," she said whilst shaking the old gentleman's hand.

8) Railway engineers often _____ through a hill to minimise the gradient.

9) The meat in the _____ 's shop window was very well displayed.

10) He was very _____ after working hard all day.   **Score** ☐ 10

Exercise 142b

11) The Cullinan is the largest diamond ever mined and has great _____ .

12) The bolt was very old and its _____ had rusted completely.

13) Their hotel room had a very _____ view over the moors.

14) The Poet Laureate writes _____ in celebration of events of national importance.

15) " _____ that you won a fortune: how would you spend the money?"

16) The magnificent _____ of *Christ of the Andes* overlooks Rio de Janeiro.

17) They walked home _____ after a long day spent in the field harvesting the crop.

18) The sentry barked out his challenge. "Halt! Who goes there? Friend or _____ ?"

19) "Try using your brain _____ of your brawn."

20) He used a ruler to _____ the width of the tube.   **Score** ☐ 10

groan	coach	toast
throat	defeat	tiger
reward	shoe	obey
obeyed	swept	crept

Exercise 143a

1) It is a simple _____ comprising two rooms downstairs and two upstairs.

2) The local _____ club organises social activities for the town's young people.

3) The Asian _____ used to be hunted and shot for trophies by big game hunters.

4) The *Titanic* was a huge _____ that was thought to be unsinkable.

5) Her nose was streaming, her head ached and her _____ was sore.

6) "If you had _____ the law, you would not be here in court," said the judge.

7) The North Atlantic fishing fleet put to sea to locate large shoals of _____ .

8) The groom asked his brother to be the best man at his _____ .

9) He hid his anxiety and appeared to be very _____ during the interview.

10) In 1665 the Great Plague of London _____ through the city.   Score [/ 10]

Exercise 143b

11) The poster offered a _____ for the capture of the notorious outlaw.

12) The grandfather clock had to be _____ every 30 days with a large key.

13) The bride's father raised his glass and proposed a _____ to the newlyweds.

14) He had worn a hole in the sole of his _____ and it was letting in water.

15) A large _____ of people had assembled to hear the politician's speech.

16) The ship's timbers could be heard to creak and _____ in the heavy seas.

17) Trying not to make a sound, she _____ slowly along the corridor.

18) The football team's _____ discussed their tactics for the forthcoming game.

19) Napoleon suffered _____ at the Battle of Waterloo in 1815.

20) "Just _____ me and stop questioning my authority!"   Score [/ 10]

Word Bank TOTAL 2,860

Across

143

7. To follow instructions or behave in accordance with a law, rule or order.
8. Cleaned a place with a broom.
9. An outer covering for the foot with a stiff sole.
10. Small edible fish with silvery scales that lives in the North Atlantic.
13. An injury in which the skin, tissue or an organ is broken by some external force with damage to the underlying tissue.
15. Past tense of 'creep'.
17. Did as told.
18. A large striped feline.

Down

1. A bus designed for long-distance travel or sightseeing.
2. A hollow receptacle, especially one that is used as a container for liquids.
3. The period of human life between childhood and maturity.
4. Something desirable given in return for what somebody has done.
5. A long, low cry expressing misery.
6. A house or other building or place in which somebody lives.
11. A number of people or things considered together or regarded as belonging together.
12. Failure to win or to realise a goal.

Down (continued)

13. A marriage ceremony, or the act of marrying.
14. Sliced bread that has been browned on both sides with heat.
15. Without anxiety or strong emotion.
16. The front part of the neck of an animal or human being.

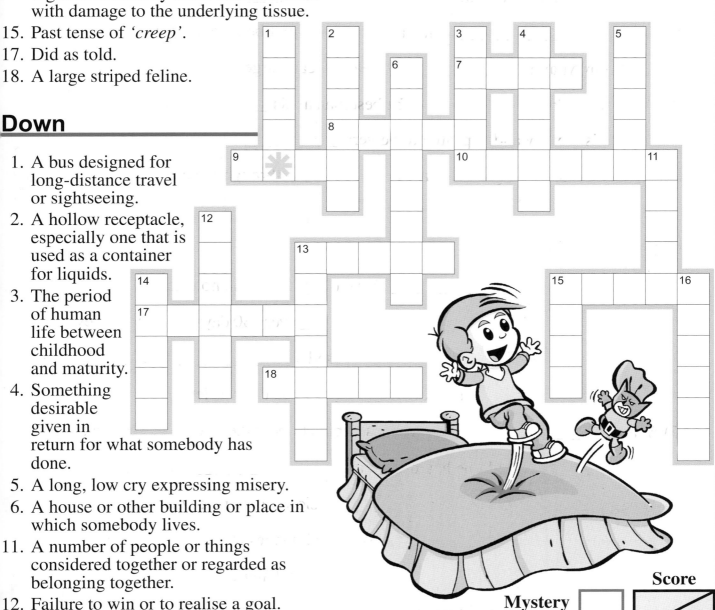

Mystery Letter [ ]

Score [/20]

prettier   **prettiest**   **beginning**
journey   **recall**   **result**
beyond   **shiver**   **demand**
deliver   **depend**   **delay**

Across

144

3. A trip or expedition from one place to another.
4. Somebody's memory or ability to remember.
8. Intended to do something.
9. The presence or absence of illnesses, injuries, or impairments.
11. Carry something to somebody.
12. A clear and firm request that is difficult to ignore or deny.
13. Having a large amount of money or possessions.
14. On the other side of something else.
15. To tremble or shake slightly because of cold, fear or illness.

Across (continued)

18. Most pleasing and charming in appearance.
19. The state of the atmosphere with regard to meteorological conditions.

Down

1. With a more attractive, pleasant face.
2. To postpone something or wait until later before doing something.
5. Tanned and dressed hide.
6. The first part or early stages of something.
7. In good physical or mental condition.
10. An individual part of a bird's plumage.
14. The air that a person or animal inhales or exhales.
16. To be affected or decided by other factors, or to vary according to the circumstances.
17. An outcome, especially the final score in a sporting competition.

Score

Mystery Letter

20

12

Exercise 144a

1) She bought a new brown _____ belt made from the finest hide.

2) "You misunderstand me. That's not quite what I _____ ."

3) Their trip was a complete disaster from _____ to end.

4) Her sister has a _____ face but she is less gifted academically.

5) She felt a _____ run down her spine as she read the horror story.

6) Good _____ is perhaps the greatest gift of all.

7) The success of the venture was _____ everyone's wildest dreams.

8) He inherited a fortune on his father's death and became very _____ overnight.

9) The manufacturer had to _____ the faulty equipment in order to repair it.

10) The _____ to their flight was caused by bad weather. **Score** ⬚ 10

Exercise 144b

11) Her garden was judged to be the _____ and she won first prize.

12) The jury returned from its deliberations to _____ the verdict.

13) He stopped running and rested for a moment in order to catch his _____ .

14) The _____ forecast for the next day was not very promising.

15) Her old aunt had a few ailments but generally remained very fit and _____ .

16) They decided to break their _____ and stay overnight in a motel.

17) The referee checked the judges' scores and announced the _____ of the contest.

18) Their latest recording is so popular that _____ has outstripped supply.

19) She uses a _____ duster to clean the higher shelves.

20) We _____ on rainfall to avert drought. **Score** ⬚ 10

fleet	screen	greedy
freedom	drown	drowned
powder	petrol	aim
claim	praise	dairy

Exercise 145a

1) He took careful _____ , released the arrow and hit the target.

2) It was a very _____ choice to make and very unexpected.

3) The doctor asked his patient to go behind the _____ and change into a gown.

4) Many herds of _____ live securely in the royal parks.

5) He had a very sweet tooth and would always _____ his pancakes in syrup.

6) The _____ led them on a conducted tour of the castle and its grounds.

7) They waved red flags and tried to _____ the train driver of the danger.

8) She likes to pamper herself after a bath and uses lots of talcum _____ .

9) He needs to _____ three additional staff to cope with the increased workload.

10) The ship foundered and many of her crew _____ .

Score [/ 10]

Exercise 145b

11) He is so _____ that he filled his plate with far more food than he could eat.

12) "We have a very distinguished _____ to speak at tonight's meeting."

13) She was full of _____ for her brother and the success that he had achieved.

14) The farmer has a large _____ herd which produces a very high milk yield.

15) He fidgeted on his chair and looked very _____ when asked if he were the culprit.

16) In the 1896 gold rush, many people raced to the Klondike to stake their _____ .

17) Many generations have fought to maintain our right to _____ of speech.

18) The price of _____ is inextricably linked to the price and supply of crude oil.

19) She tried to _____ the conversation towards a subject of her liking.

20) "He is very _____ of foot and can run like the wind."

Score [/ 10]

14

deer   **steer**
queer   **engage**
guilty   **guide**
guest   **warn**

Across

145

5. To tell somebody about something that might cause injury or harm.
6. Not usual or expected.
8. Words that express great approval or admiration.
11. Having died by immersion in water.
14. A state in which somebody is able to act and live as he or she chooses, without any undue restraints and restrictions.
16. A volatile, flammable liquid used as a fuel in internal-combustion engines.
17. A fixed or movable partition or frame that is used to conceal, divide, separate or provide shelter.
19. Responsible for a crime, wrong action or error and deserving punishment, blame or criticism.

Down

1. A young male ox.
2. A mammal distinguished by the branched antlers on males.
3. Eating to excess, or wanting to do so.
4. To lead somebody in the right direction.
7. To say, without proof or evidence, that something is true.
9. To intend or plan to do something.
10. A substance in the form of a loose grouping of many tiny dry grains.
12. Somebody who receives hospitality at the home of somebody else.
13. To die, or kill a person or animal, by immersion and usually suffocation in a liquid, normally water.
14. A group of naval ships, or a number of vehicles, boats or aircraft owned or managed as a unit.
15. A room or building where milk and cream are stored.
18. To involve somebody in an activity, or become involved or take part in an activity.

Mystery Letter   **Score** / 20

ae © 2006 Stephen Curran

season	reason	crimson
iron	medal	metal
mental	board	Briton
British	Irish	Ireland

Exercise 146a

1) He came third in the Paralympic Games event and won a bronze _____ .

2) She used many herbs and spices to _____ the exotic dish she had prepared.

3) _____ is known as the 'Emerald Isle' because of its large areas of grassland.

4) "Stop shouting, sit down quietly and _____ yourselves!"

5) The _____ Isles comprise two large islands and 5,000 smaller islands.

6) Most household _____ is buried in landfill sites.

7) Educational toys provide young children with _____ stimulation.

8) Diving into the swollen river to save the child was an act of great _____ .

9) He pulled a hamstring and had to _____ from the race.

10) The vessel slowed to allow the pilot to _____ the ship.

Score ☐ 10

Exercise 146b

11) The police negotiator tried to _____ with the leader of the hijackers.

12) She was very tired and fought to overcome an overwhelming _____ for sleep.

13) The first cast-_____ bridge was built in 1779 and it spans the River Severn.

14) High-skilled craftsmen were needed to _____ the damaged palace ceilings.

15) The _____ rails buckled and twisted in the intense heat.

16) A _____ was one of the ancient Celtic people who once lived in southern England.

17) She boarded the ferry that sailed from Liverpool across the _____ Sea to Dublin.

18) These special rules _____ only to games played during this competition.

19) "It is his own fault and he does not _____ our sympathy."

20) He was so angry that his face turned _____ .

Score ☐ 10

Across

146

1. Relating to, or carried out in, or produced by the mind.
3. Extreme courage in the face of danger or difficulty.
4. Someone who was born or brought up in, or who is a citizen of, Great Britain.
6. A flat piece of wood.
8. A deep rich red colour tinged with purple.
10. A chemical element such as copper or iron that is usually solid in form.
11. An explanation or justification for something.
13. To have a significant connection with or bearing on something.

Across (continued)

14. To return something to its proper owner, place, or condition.
16. To have earned or be worthy of something.
17. To act in a particular way that expresses general character, state or mind, or response to a situation or other people.

Down

1. A small, flat piece of metal given as an award.
2. An island situated west of Great Britain, separated by the Irish Sea.
5. A heavy, magnetic, malleable, ductile, lustrous, silvery-white metallic element used for a variety of engineering and structural products.
6. People of the United Kingdom of Great Britain and Northern Ireland.
7. To want something strongly.
9. To stop engaging in daily activities and go to bed.
12. Any one of the periods marked by particular weather conditions into which the year is traditionally divided.
13. To declare or make known a decision or intention not to do something.
15. Relating to Ireland, or its people or culture.

! Don't forget to go back to page **3** and complete ● **Oliver's Mystery Word.**

Mystery Letter

Score /20

At the Firestation

Can you find all these words in the picture below? Write the correct word against each
number. When you have finished you can colour in the picture if you want to.

axe	ladder	pole	hose-reel	leggings
fire engine	helmet	siren	extinguisher	telephone
flames	fireman	first aid kit	visor	driver

1._____   2._____   3._____

4._____   5._____   6._____

7._____   8._____   9._____

10._____   11._____   12._____

13._____   14._____   15._____

The Train Set

Can you find all these words in the picture below? Write the correct word against each number.

engine shed	tunnel	tender	signal box	locomotive
points	footbridge	switch	carriage	bogey
control box	signal	truck	buffer	flag

1._____   2._____   3._____

4._____   5._____   6._____

7._____   8._____   9._____

10._____   11._____   12._____

13._____   14._____   15._____

bathe	vase	rare
square	December	October
Germany	herd	attend
attack	wreck	wrong

Exercise 147a

1) The two friends caught several _____ on their fly-fishing weekend.

2) Mercedes-Benz, Audi and Volkswagen cars are manufactured in _____ .

3) "Go and _____ that cut with warm water to make sure it's clean."

4) The topiarist cut and shaped the long _____ into a series of arches.

5) He sat beside the fire in the inn and drank another glass of dark _____ .

6) They hoped that everyone they had invited could _____ their wedding.

7) The onset of cold weather in late _____ made a white Christmas likely.

8) The buoy with a bell warned of the _____ just below the surface of the sea.

9) He crawled gingerly to the _____ of the cliff and peered over.

10) The apple was unripe and tasted very _____ .

Score ⬛ 10

Exercise 147b

11) He failed to _____ the width accurately and scraped the car's wing on the post.

12) The Battle of Trafalgar was fought on 21st _____ 1805.

13) A very old, hand-decorated _____ , filled with flowers, stood on the huge sideboard.

14) The cub scout's mother sewed another _____ that he had earned onto his sleeve.

15) Brown bread made with wholemeal _____ is much more wholesome.

14) An open-air market is held in the town _____ every Saturday morning.

17) The farmer and his two collies managed to _____ the sheep into the pen.

18) She liked her steak well-done but he preferred his to be underdone and _____ .

19) It was a severe asthma _____ and he needed his nebuliser.

20) "We're going the _____ way. Let's turn back."

Score ⬛ 10

20

Word Bank TOTAL 2,940

Across

147

3. A powder made by grinding the edible parts of cereal grains.
6. To go to, or be present at, an event.
7. Having a tart or sharp taste.
9. A line or area that is the outermost part, or the part farthest away from the centre of something.
12. A freshwater fish that is typically smaller than the related salmon and has a speckled body.
13. A small, distinctly shaped or marked piece of fabric, metal or plastic.
15. A geometric figure with four right angles and four equal sides.
17. To destroy something completely or damage it beyond repair.
18. A large group of domestic animals.
19. Not correct or accurate.

Down

1. Swim or paddle, especially for pleasure, in an area of open water.
2. A close-set row of bushes forming a boundary in a garden, park or field.
4. Not often happening or found.
5. An open container used for displaying cut flowers or as an ornament.
8. The tenth month of the year in the Gregorian calendar.
10. The twelfth month of the year in the Gregorian calendar.
11. To try to harm somebody by using violence.
14. A federal republic, situated in Western Europe, whose capital is Berlin.
15. Thicker and heavier in body than an average person of the same height.
16. A lawyer of high rank who supervises court trials.

Put the mystery letter (✳) into the box marked **147** below. Add in the mystery letters from puzzles **148** to **153** then rearrange them to make **Kate's Mystery Word**.

The clue is **WEATHER**.

147	148	149	150	151	152	153

Mystery Word:

Now rearrange them:

Score

/20

lodge   bridge   sword
check   suit   fruit
orange   banana   member
remember   remembered   memory

Across

148

2. To examine something to establish its state or condition.
3. A set of clothes made from the same material.
5. A long and slightly curved fruit with a skin that turns from green to yellow when ripe.
8. A structure that is built above and across an obstacle allowing people or vehicles to cross it.
9. A building where goods are manufactured on a large scale.
10. Somebody who belongs to and participates in a particular group.
11. A gatekeeper's small house.
12. A storey of a building that is wholly or partly below ground level.

Across (continued)

16. Past tense of 'wear'.
17. To roll smoothly along the ground or some other flat surface.
18. To recall something to mind.

Down

1. Used to introduce doubt regarding two equal possibilities.
4. A paved path for pedestrians alongside a street.
6. Retained something in the memory without forgetting it.
7. A pigment or dye that is a mixture of red and yellow.
9. An edible part of a plant.
13. A long-bladed hand-held weapon.
14. The ability to retain knowledge.
15. To gain a point or points in a match or game.
16. Introduces a question asking about the name or identity of a person or people.

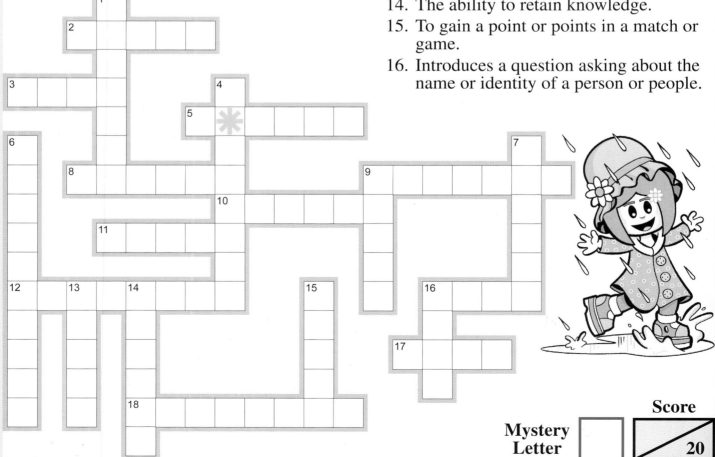

Mystery Letter ☐

Score ◧ 20

wore	**score**
whom	**whether**
bowl	**factory**
basement	**pavement**

Word Bank
TOTAL
2,960

Exercise 148a

1) The golfer holed the putt, retrieved his ball and filled out his _____ card.

2) She asked him to _____ the figures and confirm that the total was correct.

3) She was very upset that he had not _____ that it was her birthday.

4) He worked in a _____ that manufactured furniture.

5) "I want to _____ a formal complaint with the council and hand in this petition."

6) Spending a summer holiday on the beach does not _____ everyone.

7) Eating lots of fresh _____ and vegetables provides you with many vitamins.

8) The _____ outside her house was icy and dangerous to walk on.

9) His dilemma was _____ or not to offer them advice.

10) He _____ a top hat and tails for the investiture ceremony.   **Score** ◪ 10

Exercise 148b

11) Try as she might, she could not _____ the teacher's name.

12) *Excalibur* was the magic _____ given to King Arthur by the Lady of the Lake.

13) Every _____ of Parliament filed through the division lobbies to vote.

14) They sheltered down in the _____ while the hurricane raged outside.

15) The _____ 's skin had turned from green to yellow as it ripened.

14) "To _____ should I make this cheque payable?" he asked.

17) She had a good _____ for faces but she forgot people's names.

18) The ball struck him between the eyes, right on the _____ of his nose.

19) It was a cold morning, so he ate a large _____ of porridge for breakfast.

20) The Belisha beacon's _____ lights flashed in the gloom.   **Score** ◪ 10

using	during	duty
truth	eight	weight
weigh	dumb	figure
scripture	creature	entertain

Exercise 149a

1) It was a poor _____ and the explanation she gave was unacceptable.

2) At the front of the orchestra stood a magnificent grand _____ with its lid raised.

3) The unicorn is a mythical _____ that resembles a horse with a single horn.

4) He worked for twelve hours: from 7.45am until a quarter to _____ that evening.

5) His research was deemed unimportant and did not _____ in the final report.

6) He enjoyed travelling all over London _____ his bus pass.

7) He had been responsible for their safety and had to _____ the blame.

8) The _____ was read by a member of the church's congregation.

9) It was too small and the shop agreed to _____ it for a larger one.

10) The bough broke under the _____ of the snow.

Score [/ 10]

Exercise 149b

11) Despite being _____ since birth, he had learned to speak intelligibly.

12) Popular singers and comedians _____ the armed forces stationed overseas.

13) The Customs officer charged him _____ on the camera that he had bought abroad.

14) The milk was rancid and she had to _____ it away.

15) Everyone had been collected from school _____ one boy who waited in vain.

16) "Take your time, _____ up all the options and tell me which you prefer."

17) She started coughing uncontrollably _____ the performance and had to leave.

18) His creditors threatened to take him to _____ to recover their money.

19) A _____ wave broke over him and swept him towards the beach.

20) If you tell the _____ , you have nothing to fear.

Score [/ 10]

pour	court
shoulder	huge
exchange	except
excuse	piano

Word Bank
TOTAL
2,980

Across

149

3. Any living person or animal.
8. Something that corresponds to fact or reality.
10. To amuse or interest a person or audience.
11. Very big in size or amount.
12. The cardinal number denoting one more than seven.
16. The place where an arm attaches to the trunk.
17. To make a substance flow in a stream.
18. A symbol representing something other than a letter of the alphabet, especially a number.
19. A word indicating the only person or thing that does not apply to a statement just made.

Down

1. The sacred writings of the Bible.
2. An open space surrounded with buildings and walls.
4. A large musical instrument with a keyboard.
5. Something that somebody is obliged to do for moral, legal or religious reasons.
6. To find out the weight of somebody or something.
7. The heaviness of somebody or something.
9. Employing something for some purpose.
12. To give something and receive something different in return.
13. Throughout a particular period or event.
14. To release somebody from blame or criticism for a mistake or wrongdoing.
15. Unable to speak.

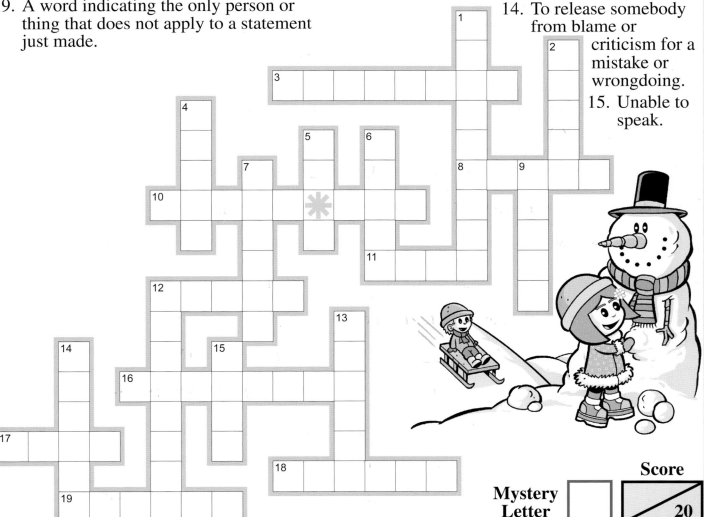

Mystery Letter

Score / 20

reply	drying	carrying
foggy	worship	worse
worst	worry	city
cities	circle	palace

Across

150

2. A piece of metal money.
3. Becoming dry.
5. Less good than something else.
8. Something that indicates the presence of something or somebody.
9. Very unclear or vague.
10. A mythological very tall or large creature, usually similar to a human in shape.
13. To respond to what somebody has said.
15. A very large town where large numbers of people live and work.
17. An incorrect, unwise, or unfortunate act or decision caused by bad judgment or lack of information or care.
18. A curved line surrounding a centre point, every point of the line being an equal distance from the centre point.

Down

1. Plural of 'city'.
2. Taking something you are holding to another place.
4. Making a loud and annoying racket.
5. Least good, most unpleasant, or most unfavourable.
6. A machine that converts energy into mechanical power or motion.
7. To treat somebody or something as divine.
11. An action, gesture or sign used as a means of communication.
12. To separate or split into two or more parts.
14. A grand and imposing building that is the official residence of a sovereign.
16. To feel anxious or to cause another person to feel anxious.

Score

Mystery Letter

20

© 2006 Stephen Curran

Exercise 150a

1) The two cars are so alike that it is easy to ___Mistake___ one for the other.

2) *A Tale of Two* ___giants___ is a classic novel by Charles Dickens.

3) They go to Sunday ___Palace___ at church every week.

4) She invited her brother and his wife to dinner but she has not yet received a ___coin___ .

5) He wrote and dated the cheque but forgot to ___sign___ it, so it could not be cashed.

6) The air outside is damp and still and the washing on the line is not ___drying___ .

7) A tsunami is a ___noisy___ ocean wave caused by an underwater earthquake.

8) The parking meter rejected the ___signal___ and she did not have another 50p piece.

9) They waited for the weather to improve but it just got ___worse___ .

10) He checked the oil level in the ___engine___ and added a litre. **Score** [/ 10]

Exercise 150b

11) Many people may be ___Carrying___ a virus without knowing it.

12) "Her biggest ___worry___ while she was in hospital was who would feed her cats!"

13) *Concorde* was a spectacular aircraft but its engines were extremely ___noisy___ .

14) They waited for the ___city___ and, when they saw it, they began their attack.

15) "We have excellent seats in the theatre in the front row of the dress ___giant___ ."

14) It is very ___noisy___ on the motorway, with visibility down to only twenty metres.

17) The judge said that it was the ___worst___ case of its kind that he had ever seen.

18) She used a large knife to cut the cake and ___divide___ it into equal portions.

19) Many important financial institutions are situated in the ___city___ of London.

20) The British parliament sits in the ___Palace___ of Westminster. **Score** [/ 10]

earnest	search	French
honest	seldom	quite
wicked	selfish	throne
choke	clothes	owe

Exercise 151a

1) She has a large extended _____ with many great-grandchildren.

2) He performed the task so many times that it became _____ nature to him.

3) His _____ words conveyed the gravity of the situation.

4) *The Emperor's New* _____ is a fable that teaches us not to be easily deceived.

5) Queen Elizabeth II came to the _____ on the death of her father in 1952.

6) He pulled out the _____ , turned the key and started the engine.

7) The low-lying _____ of land was flooded when the river burst its banks.

8) Although he is in constant pain, he _____ complains about it.

9) The inventor made a fortune from a clever _____ that he patented.

10) He would tease people with his _____ sense of humour. **Score** ◸ 10

Exercise 151b

11) A mountain rescue service _____ party located the missing climbers.

12) "I sent the cheque _____ days ago and you should have received it by now."

13) He has a reputation for being trustworthy and as _____ as the day is long.

14) They traded in their car for a _____ carrier to transport their five children.

15) They thought the film was _____ good, but not as good as the book.

16) She lived in Paris for many years and learned to speak _____ fluently.

17) He remortgaged his house and spent a small _____ on improvements.

18) The council announces all planning applications in the _____ newspaper.

19) He is very _____ and thinks of no-one but himself.

20) I _____ my school teachers a great debt of gratitude. **Score** ◸ 10

28

ae

area	idea
family	people
local	several
second	fortune

Word Bank TOTAL 3,020

Across

151

7. A large amount of financial wealth or material possessions.
9. Garments that cover the body.
11. Rarely, not often.
12. Intensely serious and sincere in manner or attitude.
14. A personal opinion or belief.
16. Very wrong or very bad.
17. The 60th part of a minute of time.
18. The measurement of a surface.

Down

1. The language of France.
2. To be under an obligation to pay or repay an amount of money.
3. Relating to, situated in, or providing a service for a particular area.

Down (continued)

4. Never cheating, lying, or breaking the law.
5. Somewhat, entirely, or nearly.
6. An ornate chair occupied by a monarch or bishop on ceremonial occasions.
8. A group of people who are closely related by birth, marriage or adoption.
9. To stop breathing, or breathe with great difficulty, because of a blockage or restriction of the throat.
10. To look into, over, or through something carefully in order to find something or somebody.
11. Concerned with your own interests, needs and wishes while ignoring those of others.
13. Various or separate.
15. Human beings considered collectively or in general.

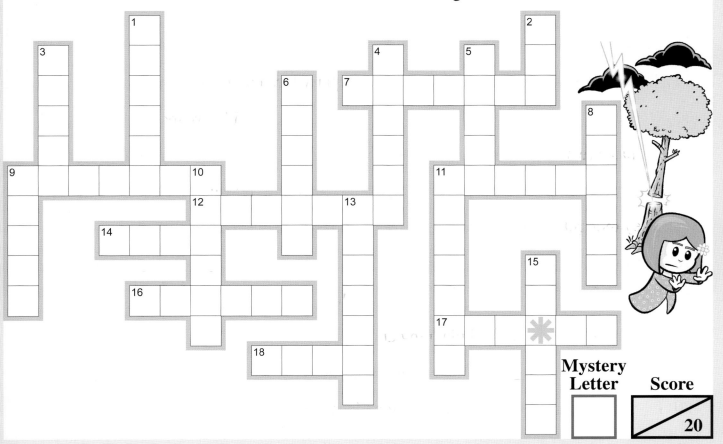

Mystery Letter

Score

20

cruel	Tuesday	Wednesday
disgust	picnic	arithmetic
flood	wooden	aunt
saucer	farewell	else

Across

5. The upright or turned-over neckband of a coat, jacket, dress, shirt or blouse.
7. The third day of the week.
9. Used to refer in a vague way to somebody or something other or different.
11. Any of several small horse breeds.
12. Deliberately and remorselessly causing pain or anguish.
13. The branch of a country's armed forces that crews, maintains, and fights on warships.
14. Made or consisting of wood.
17. An expression of good wishes at parting.
18. Moving, said, or done awkwardly.
19. The branch of mathematics that deals with addition, subtraction, multiplication and division.

152

Down

1. Sacred, saintly, pure, consecrated, or awe-inspiring.
2. A large expanse of salt water, especially any of the Earth's five main seas.
3. The second day of the week.
4. Somebody's mother's or father's sister, or somebody's uncle's wife.
6. Failing to win a victory.
8. A small, shallow dish designed to hold a matching cup.
10. A very large amount of water that has overflowed from a source such as a river or a broken pipe onto a previously dry area.
11. An informal meal prepared for eating in the open air.
15. A feeling of horrified or sickened distaste for something.
16. A thin cylindrical instrument used for drawing or writing.

Mystery Letter ☐   Score ◻ 20

pencil	ocean
collar	clumsy
holy	pony
navy	losing

Exercise 152a

1) Much to her _____ , she was asked to help clean up the mess.

2) He was very _____ and kept knocking things over.

3) He poured the slopped tea back into the cup from the _____ .

4) Many shops used to close for a half-day on a _____ .

5) He joined the merchant _____ from college and rose to the rank of captain.

6) "Calm down and don't get so hot under the _____ !"

7) The cooper made and repaired _____ barrels to hold sherry and port wine.

8) Jerusalem is the _____ City of the Jews and the sacred city of Christians and Moslems.

9) She has a very poor sense of direction and is always _____ her way.

10) "_____ me in provisionally for a meeting next week."   **Score** [/ 10]

Exercise 152b

11) Global warming is thought to affect the Gulf Stream in the Atlantic _____ .

12) They took a hamper and a rug and travelled out to the country for a _____ .

13) The average of several numbers is known as the ' _____ mean'.

14) The Spanish Inquisition used very _____ methods to extract confessions.

15) She went to bed late on _____ and got up early on Wednesday morning.

16) The _____ express was a system of carrying mail using a relay of horses and riders.

17) His sister was pleased to become an _____ on the birth of his son.

18) The proposed development gave rise to a _____ of complaints from the residents.

19) He wished his friend _____ and watched the train depart.

20) "I'm warning you. Bring it here tomorrow or _____ !"   **Score** [/ 10]

ae © 2006 Stephen Curran

catalogue	**spacious**	**unconscious**
vicious	**atrocious**	**gnashed**
gnomon	**gnome**	**gnarled**
superstitious	**infectious**	**conscientious**

Exercise 153a

1) The railway disaster was caused by a _____ of errors.

2) The leaning tower of Pisa is far from _____ .

3) The shadow cast by a sundial's _____ indicates the time of day.

4) A _____ month is the time between one new moon and the next: about 29.5 days.

5) People who are _____ believe that Friday 13th is unlucky.

6) "It's completely _____ for you to help me. I can manage on my own!"

7) The people next door never speak and are most _____ .

8) Many dictators have committed _____ crimes and acts of violence.

9) He _____ his teeth in pain as they lifted him onto the stretcher.

10) The old fisherman's hands were _____ and calloused. **Score** [/ 10]

Exercise 153b

11) He trains very hard to maintain both his fitness and his _____ physique.

12) It was a _____ and unprovoked attack on two individuals.

13) His knee was dislocated and his lower leg lay at an _____ angle.

14) The lounge was very _____ with plenty of room for all their furniture.

15) The treatment and disposal of by-products from _____ reactors causes concern.

16) She slipped _____ into the room and surprised them all.

17) _____ objectors are opposed to being enlisted to fight in a war.

18) The severe blow to his head rendered him _____ .

19) She had a very _____ laugh and soon everyone was laughing with her.

20) A garden _____ with a fishing rod was sitting by the pond. **Score** [/ 10]

lunar
nuclear
unnoticed
unnatural

perpendicular
muscular
unnecessary
unneighbourly

**Word Bank
TOTAL
3,060**

Across

153

1. Roomy and containing ample space.
3. The arm of a sundial.
4. Not seen or spotted by anybody.
6. Physically strong and with well-developed muscles.
10. Relating to the nucleus of an atom.
14. Contrary to the physical laws of nature.
15. A tiny supernatural being.
16. Showing fierce violence, dangerously aggressive, or intending to do harm.
17. Relating to a moon or its movement around a planet.
18. Appallingly bad, extremely evil or cruel.
19. Teeth ground together.

Down

2. Thorough and diligent in performing a task.
4. Not essential, needed, or required.
5. Convinced that performing or not performing certain actions brings good or bad luck.
7. Experiencing a loss of senses, or unaware of something.
8. Perfectly vertical.
9. Not friendly, helpful, or kind.
11. A list of goods for sale.
12. Twisted and full of knots.
13. Causing infection.

! Don't forget to go back to page **20** and complete **Kate's Mystery Word.**

Mystery Letter

Score

/20

ae © 2006 Stephen Curran

33

At the Circus

Can you find all these words in the picture below? Write the correct word against each number.

clown	safety net	juggler	fire eater	ringmaster
club	trampoline	top hat	spotlight	bumper
leotard	catcher	big top	somersault	circus ring

1._____   2._____   3._____

4._____   5._____   6._____

7._____   8._____   9._____

10._____   11._____   12._____

13._____   14._____   15._____

© 2006 Stephen Curran

On the Village Green

Can you find all these words in the picture below? Write the correct word against each number. When you have finished you can colour in the picture if you want to.

wicket	**thatch**	**hamper**	**duck**	**bandstand**
footpath	**porch**	**fielder**	**kite**	**drum**
bench	**football**	**lead**	**pond**	**bowler**

1._____ 2._____ 3._____

4._____ 5._____ 6._____

7._____ 8._____ 9._____

10._____ 11._____ 12._____

13._____ 14._____ 15._____

dinghy	pennant	life-jacket
mainsail	oars	buoy
jib	tiller	architecture
overture	literature	aerodrome

Exercise 154a

1) An artist's detailed _____ enhanced the newspaper report.

2) The small _____ at Heston developed into London's Heathrow airport.

3) The divers found the wreck and marked its location with a _____ on the surface.

4) He pushed the _____ to starboard and the boat turned to port.

5) A tank has _____ tracks to enable it to cross any terrain.

6) Some _____ sprays contain CFCs that may damage the Earth's ozone layer.

7) Charles Dickens contributed greatly to 19th Century English _____ .

8) A small, colourful _____ flew from the top of the ships mast.

9) No political party won an _____ majority in the election.

10) He put the _____ into the rowlocks.

Score [/ 10]

Exercise 154b

11) In 1909, Louis Blériot piloted the first _____ to cross the English Channel.

12) The *William Tell* _____ was composed by Gioacchino Antonio Rossini.

13) She put the _____ in her mouth and sucked it while holding the stick.

14) The *Red Arrows* are the Royal Air Force's _____ display team.

15) The _____ unfurled from the yard and the sailing ship got underway.

16) A _____ is stowed under each passenger's seat on commercial aircraft.

17) They used an inflatable _____ with an outboard engine as the yacht's tender.

18) A huge _____ cleared a way through the rubble after the earthquake.

19) The yacht's crew raced forward to replace the damaged _____ .

20) The great pyramids exemplify Egyptian _____ .

Score [/ 10]

36

aerosol	aerobatics
aeroplane	overall
lollipop	bulldozer
caterpillar	illustration

Word Bank TOTAL 3,080

Across

154

2. A picture that accompanies text.
6. A handle, attached to the rudder, for steering a small boat.
8. A large anchored float that serves as a guide or warning to ships.
13. A triangular flag.
15. A small airfield with limited facilities.
16. A container with gas under pressure.
19. Written works with artistic value.
20. From one extremity to another.

Down

1. A small rowing boat or ship's tender.
3. The lava of a butterfly or moth.
4. The art and science of designing and constructing buildings.
5. A large boiled sweet fixed onto a stick.
7. A jacket made of buoyant material.
9. An opening or opportunity.
10. The largest and most important sail on a sailing ship.
11. A construction vehicle with tracks and a wide blade used for moving earth.
12. Stunt flying of an aircraft.
14. A powered flying vehicle with wings.
17. Wooden poles with one broad flat end, used to propel a boat.
18. A small, foremost triangular sail.

Put the mystery letter (✱) into the box marked **154** below. Add in the mystery letters from puzzles **155** to **161** then rearrange them to make **Dickens's Mystery Word**.

The clue is **DWELLING**.

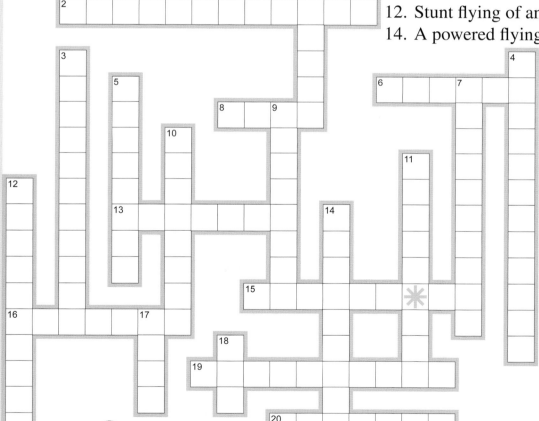

154	155	156	157	158	159	160	161

Now rearrange them:

Mystery Word:

Score / 20

© 2006 Stephen Curran

37

parallel	plimsolls	penicillin
millionaire	cellophane	christen
chasm	chiropodist	chlorine
chemistry	Christianity	chrysalis

Across

155

1. Someone trained in the care and treatment of feet.
7. A member of a chorus, choir or other group of singers.
8. The religion based on the life, teachings and example of Jesus Christ.
10. A plant with brightly coloured globe-shaped flowers and small densely clustered petals.
13. The hard cocoon that protects a pupa during its change from larva to adult.
16. An instrument for measuring electric current in amperes.
17. Always the same distance apart.
18. A tough, transparent, paper-like wrapping material made from viscose.

Down

2. Light canvas shoes with a rubber sole.
3. An instrument to measure temperature.
4. Visually pleasing.
5. An antibiotic originally derived from mould.
6. Distorted, especially in a strange or disturbing way.
8. The study of the structure, composition, properties, and reactive characteristics of substances.
9. A gaseous, poisonous, corrosive, greenish-yellow chemical used to kill germs.
10. A bluish-white hard metallic element.
11. Somebody whose net worth or income is more than one million pounds, or other unit of currency.
12. A small printed form which, when filled in and signed, instructs a bank to pay a specified sum of money to the person named on it.
14. To make somebody, especially a baby, a member of the Christian church.
15. A deep crack or hole in the ground.

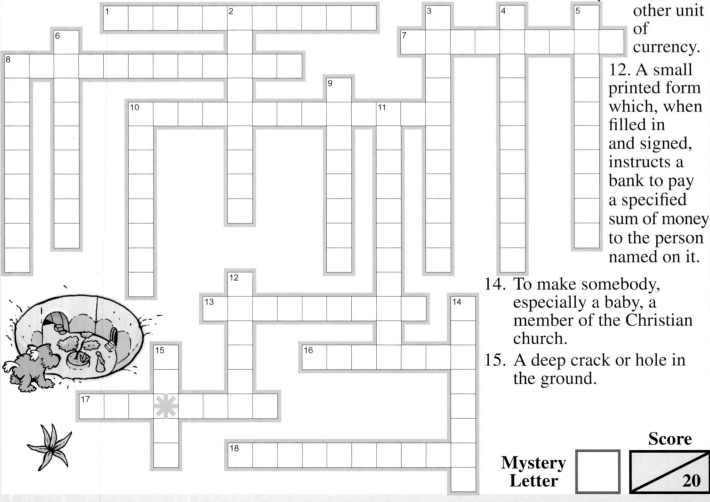

Mystery Letter ☐

Score ⬜/20

38

chorister	chromium	
chrysanthemum	grotesque	Word Bank
picturesque	cheque	TOTAL
thermometer	ammeter	3,100

Exercise 155a

1) The mercury in the _____ indicated only two degrees Celsius.

2) The florist sold bouquets of flowers wrapped in _____ .

3) She auditioned and was accepted as a _____ in the Cathedral's choir.

4) There was a special _____ between them and they worked together well.

5) Although they are _____ , railway tracks appear to converge into the distance.

6) Metals electroplated with _____ are more resistant to corrosion.

7) The mountaineers used ladders to cross a deep _____ blocking their path.

8) The village is very _____ and has been painted by many artists.

9) The electrician's _____ showed the current to be 50 amps.

10) "You may write a _____ or pay by credit card."   Score [/ 10]

Exercise 155b

11) The Greek name for the _____ literally means *golden flower*.

12) Missionaries still work to spread _____ throughout the world.

13) Gargoyles with _____ features look down from the guttering.

14) The water in the swimming baths smelled strongly of _____ .

15) She made an appointment with the _____ for a pedicure.

16) The young children carried their PE kit and _____ to school in a bag.

17) Butterfly and moth pupae are protected by a _____ or a hard cocoon.

18) He sold his business for a small fortune and became a multi-_____ .

19) They asked the vicar to _____ their baby daughter.

20) Sir Alexander Fleming discovered _____ in 1928.   Score [/ 10]

barometer	voltmeter	altimeter
speedometer	accent	accessory
accelerate	metre	centimetre
millimetre	kilometre	level-crossing

Exercise 156a

1) The locomotive's brakes failed and it hit the _____ at the end of the track.

2) They were so close that there was hardly a _____ between them.

3) The _____ gates closed as the express train approached.

4) The man in the _____ pulled the lever and the points changed.

5) She was born in Newcastle and spoke with a strong Northern _____ .

6) The _____ showed the pilot that he was flying at 15,000 feet.

7) He used a _____ to check the amount of power in the car battery.

8) A tall _____ on brick columns carried the railway across the narrow valley.

9) The baby had grown a _____ in the last five weeks.

10) Every squirrel buries a _____ of nuts to eat in the winter.   Score [/10]

Exercise 156b

11) Fertilisers are added to crops to nourish them and to _____ their growth.

12) The car's _____ confirmed that he was driving within the speed limit.

13) He was a _____ at the school and only returned home for the holidays.

14) 'Ghost' trains are run during winter nights to keep the _____ and points free from ice.

15) A limerick is a five-line humorous poem with regular _____ and rhyme patterns.

16) Although many think that he is _____ , he does respect others' beliefs.

17) She has an _____ desire for fame that governs the way she lives her life.

18) When the _____ shows falling pressure, it indicates unsettled weather.

19) Two and a half times around the running track is one _____ .

20) By helping the criminal escape, he became an _____ .   Score [/10]

Across

156

3. Having supreme unquestionable power over everything.
9. A basic unit of length.
10. An instrument that continuously measures and displays a vehicle's speed.
12. To go, or cause something to move faster.
13. Someone who pays for a room, and usually daily meals, in a private home or boarding house.
15. A bridge that usually takes a road or railway over a wide valley.
16. An instrument that measures voltage.
17. A unit of length equal to one hundredth of a metre.
18. Lacking in, or opposed to, any religious faith.
19. The steel bars of a railway track.

Down

1. A unit of length equal to one thousandth of a metre.
2. A building from which a stretch of railway track is controlled.
4. 1,000 metres.
5. An optional part.
6. An instrument measuring changes in atmospheric pressure.
7. A pair of spring-loaded or hydraulic pads attached to both ends of rolling stock or at the end of a railway track.
8. The manner of pronunciation.
11. A place where a road crosses a railway line.
12. An instrument that shows height above sea level.
14. To collect and store a large quantity of something.

Mystery Letter

Score

20

© 2006 Stephen Curran

41

irrigation	irresponsible	irritable
athletics	philately	gymnastics
skin-diving	mountaineering	karate
yachting	electronics	archaeology

Across

157

1. The scientific study of ancient cultures through the examination of their material remains.
5. Track-and-field events.
6. The art, hobby or profession of producing pictures with a camera.
9. Not having or showing any care for the consequences of personal actions.
12. One behind another.
15. The sport or pastime of sailing in a yacht.
17. Underwater diving using flippers, mask and snorkel.
19. Any method used to supply water to a dry area in order to help crops grow.
20. A three-wheeled vehicle driven by pedals or a motor.

Down

2. The scientific study of the universe.
3. An object, usually glass, plastic or metal, that reflects light.
4. Stamp collecting.
7. The branch of zoology that deals with the scientific study of birds.
8. Collectable decorative or household objects which are valued because of their age.
10. The technology of electronic devices.
11. Easily annoyed or exasperated.
13. The sport or pastime of climbing mountains.
14. The activity of exploring holes and shafts formed naturally in limestone regions and the underground caves connected to them.
16. Physical training using equipment such as bars, rings and vaulting horses.
18. A traditional Japanese form of unarmed combat.

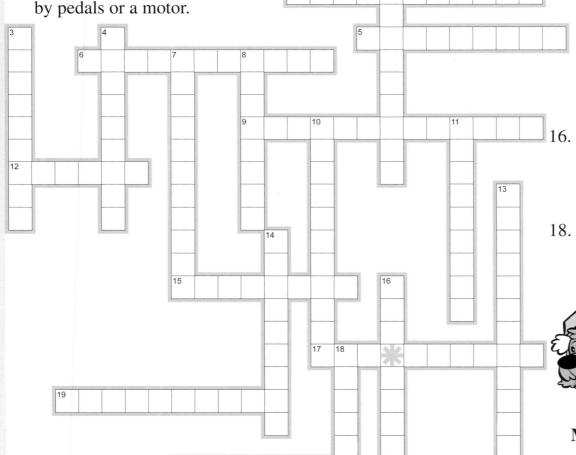

Mystery Letter

Score

20

© 2006 Stephen Curran ae

ornithology	antiques
pot-holing	astronomy
photography	tandem
tricycle	reflector

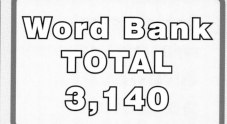

Word Bank
TOTAL
3,140

Exercise 157a

1) She is very interested in _____ and goes bird-watching every weekend.

2) "His interest in _____ has enabled him to fill six stamp albums."

3) They decided to share a _____ rather than cycle separately.

4) Modern _____ produces digital images rather than images on film.

5) He trained as an _____ engineer and works on microprocessors.

6) Galileo's work on the telescope contributed greatly to _____ .

7) They bought a mask and snorkel and went _____ in the lagoon.

8) _____ has taught us much about ancient civilisations.

9) He could break a roof tile with a _____ chop using the side of his open hand.

10) She enjoyed _____ and exploring underground caves. **Score** ◻10

Exercise 157b

11) Her favourite events in _____ are the high jump and the long jump.

12) "Your bicycle should be fitted with a _____ in case your lights fail."

13) Cowes week is a festival of _____ with many races for sailing boats.

14) He was fractious and grew more _____ as his tiredness and hunger increased.

15) When he outgrew his _____ , he learned to ride a bicycle.

16) The views can be spectacular but _____ is a very high-risk sport.

17) "It was very _____ to just wander off without telling us!"

18) She had collected many valuable 18th and 19th Century _____ .

19) He excelled at two events in _____ : the vault and the parallel bars.

20) The Archimedean screw raised water for use in _____ . **Score** ◻10

lubricate	efficient	pneumatic
maintenance	enamel	milometer
tyre-lever	moustache	colonel
parachute	pageant	khaki

Exercise 158a

1) The system designed to _____ the moving parts failed and they seized up.

2) He prised the tyre from the wheel rim with a _____ .

3) He carefully trimmed his _____ , then he shaved the rest of his face.

4) Modern condensing boilers make _____ use of gas.

5) The coronation of a new monarch is a colourful and spectacular _____ .

6) After free-falling 8,000 feet, his _____ opened and he floated down.

7) In World War II, the German uniform was grey and the British wore _____ .

8) His eyes are not looking in parallel but new glasses should correct the _____ .

9) The crown of a tooth is protected by a layer of thin, hard _____ .

10) It was a cold night, so she put a thick _____ on the bed.

Score ☐ / 10

Exercise 158b

11) "Don't rush along the corridor and _____ into other people!"

12) He filled his water pistol and began to _____ his friends.

13) The car salesman could not verify that the _____ reading was correct.

14) The workmen were digging up the road using a _____ drill.

15) The wildebeests were startled by the lioness and began to _____ .

16) Gas appliances require regular _____ to operate efficiently and safely.

17) "The birth of _____ gave them four times the pleasure and four times the work!"

18) The lease had expired and the tenants were given two weeks to _____ the property.

19) He fetched some more coal to _____ up the fire.

20) He was promoted from _____ to brigadier.

Score ☐ / 10

44

Across

158

1. A large-scale play representing historical or legendary events.
3. A glassy decorative or protective coating.
5. To apply an oily or greasy substance to something in order to reduce friction to moving parts.
8. A bed cover made of two layers of fabric stitched together, with interior padding.
9. A rigid bar used to remove a tyre from the rim of a wheel.
10. Operated by compressed air in a tool or machine.
13. A shortened word for quadruplets, quadrangles, quadrats or quadriceps.

Across (continued)

15. To partly close the eyes so as to see better.
16. To give up, leave or resign.
17. Facial hair on the upper lip.
19. A dull, brownish-yellow colour.

Down

2. Performing tasks in an organised and capable way.
4. Repair work that is done regularly.
6. A canopy for slowing the speed of fall of a person or an object from an aircraft.
7. A military rank in the British Army.
11. A long, narrow, flat-bottomed boat used for transporting freight on rivers and canals.
12. A distance-recording device in a vehicle.
14. To force something out through a narrow opening in a strong quick stream.
15. An uncontrolled headlong rush of frightened animals.
18. To add fuel to a fire and stir it up to make it burn more intensely.

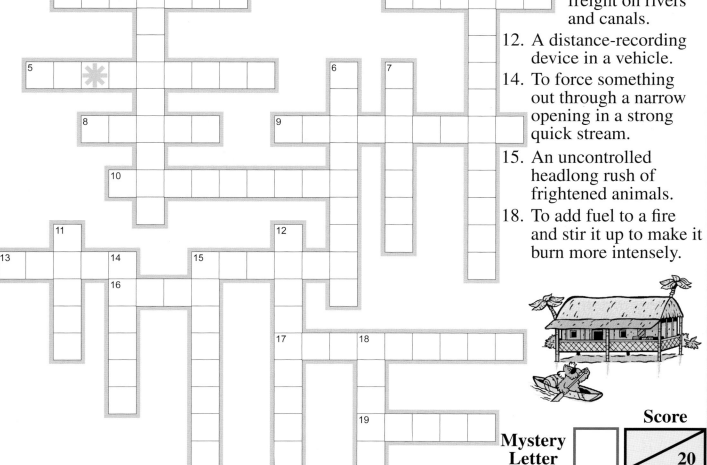

Mystery Letter

Score

/20

stretcher   cygnet   scaffold
scamper   scampi   swamp
swap   swarm   swipe
tweezers   twig   twine

Across

159

5. An exchange of one thing for another.
7. Held something firmly and tightly in position.
10. To beg or borrow without intending to make repayment or return.
11. String or cord made from threads or strands that have been twisted together.
13. To hit somebody or something with a forceful swinging or sweeping blow.
14. Waste material.
15. A miser.
16. A large group of insects in flight.
17. To submerge an area in water.

Down

1. A small plucking or holding instrument.
2. Plant material such as straw or rushes used as roofing on a house.
3. Fried prawn tails.
4. A young or baby swan.
5. To run quickly or playfully.
6. A device for carrying somebody in a lying position who is sick or injured.
8. To make somebody temporarily unable to see.
9. A small branch or shoot.
12. Used to show that one number or amount is added to another.
13. A framework of poles and planks for supporting workers.
14. A small marine crustacean with ten legs, a fan-shaped tail, and a pair of pincers.

Score

Mystery Letter

/20

clamped	thatch
scrap	scrooge
scrounge	dazzle
plus	shrimp

Word Bank TOTAL 3,180

Exercise 159a

1) The story of the *Ugly Duckling* is about a _____ that becomes a beautiful swan.

2) "We have chicken in a basket or, if you prefer seafood, we have _____ ."

3) The _____ on the cottage roof was leaking and needed renewing.

4) The shop assistant tried to _____ his credit card but it was damaged.

5) "That chocolate looks delicious. Can I _____ just a small piece from you?"

6) The St. John Ambulance crew carried the injured footballer on a _____ .

7) They use a _____ boat, powered by an aeroplane propeller, to explore the wetlands.

8) The little girl, fishing in a rock pool with a net, caught a _____ .

9) Charles I climbed the _____ , addressed the crowd and knelt for his execution.

10) The cost of the work was £30.00 _____ £6.00 VAT.

Score 10

Exercise 159b

11) She _____ her hand across her mouth to stop herself from screaming.

12) The dry _____ snapped with a loud crack when he trod on it.

13) It was a joy to see his grandson _____ to the front gate to greet him.

14) His mother used a pair of _____ to remove the splinter from his finger.

15) His masterstroke was to _____ the judges with a triple somersault.

16) A _____ of gnats hung in the air like a dark cloud.

17) "It's time you were less of a _____ and bought some sweets of your own!"

18) He is a keen collector and will _____ his spare stamps with other collectors.

19) She had too much to do and had to _____ her plans for the weekend.

20) She tied back the shrubs using green gardening _____ .

Score 10

ae © 2006 Stephen Curran
47

sprint	dizzy	slippery
twirl	drake	twitter
wage	supporter	tweet
swindle	whizzed	sprawl

Exercise 160a

1) After a long race, it finally came down to a _____ for the line.

2) The galleon called into port to take on _____ of fresh fruit and water.

3) The _____ mallard is much more brightly coloured than the female.

4) She saves all she can whereas her brother tends to _____ his money.

5) There are still many _____ in life that have no plausible explanation.

6) The town has developed in a haphazard way and become an urban _____ .

7) The team with the _____ points is relegated to a lower division.

8) She tried to stay awake but, finally, she had to _____ to sleep.

9) The Egyptian pharaoh began to _____ war on the Hittites.

10) The bullets _____ by only narrowly missing him.   **Score** ⧄ **10**

Exercise 160b

11) He conceived a cunning deception to _____ her out of a vast sum of money.

12) The path was covered with ice and very _____ .

13) She felt very _____ and the room seemed to spin around her.

14) He could see the bird sitting in the tree and hear its high pitched _____ .

15) They could not contain their _____ and the urge to laugh out loud.

16) The baby watched the mobile over her cot _____ around.

17) "Why don't you stop being a _____ and do something useful for a change!"

18) The dentist told her to use a _____ with harder bristles.

19) Newly-hatched chicks _____ noisily and constantly.

20) He is a keen _____ of the local football team.   **Score** ⧄ **10**

mirth	fewest
mysteries	toothbrush
squander	nuisance
succumb	supplies

Across

160

1. To give in.
3. To sit or lie with the arms and legs spread awkwardly in different directions.
4. To obtain something from somebody, especially money, by deception or fraud.
9. A light, high-pitched note made by a bird.
10. A short, swift race.
12. The least in number.
16. To spin round quickly.
17. To spend or use something precious in a wasteful and extravagant way.
19. Gives, sells or provides.

Down

1. Sliding easily from the grasp.
2. Puzzling events or situations.
5. A payment for work.
6. A male duck.
7. Somebody who supports a cause, person, idea, course of action, political party, or sports team.
8. To sing in a succession of light, high-pitched chirping sounds.
11. A small brush for cleaning the teeth.
13. Moved or travelled somewhere rapidly.
14. An annoying or irritating person or thing.
15. Happiness or enjoyment, especially accompanied by laughter.
18. Unsteady, as if about to lose balance, and slightly giddy.

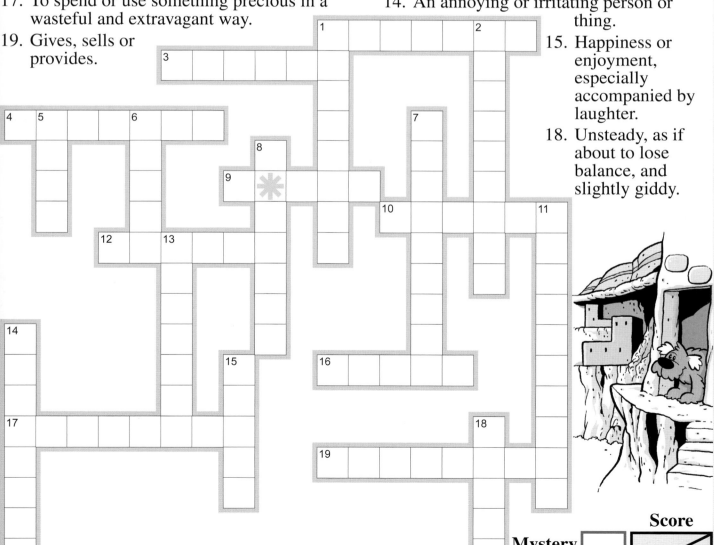

Mystery Letter

Score

/20

ae © 2006 Stephen Curran

patches	**forgeries**	**counted**
entries	**clutch**	**quartz**
rip	**suiting**	**ripping**
sadder	**towbar**	**hatched**

Exercise 161a

1) It was a very __________ orange and she found it very refreshing.

2) The bank notes were ______________ but difficult to distinguish from genuine ones.

3) "Please move away from here and find __________________ else to play!"

4) "It will be the ____________ day this year with temperatures in the 80s."

5) She was very upset by the report but even ____________ news was to follow.

6) They hitched the caravan to the car's ____________ and drove off the campsite.

7) The __________________ of five bars of chocolate from a total of six leaves only one.

8) The winner was announced when all the votes had been _______________ .

9) "It was very hard to pick an appropriate piece of music ______________ the occasion."

10) The miners worked with lamps in the _____________ of tunnels.

Score /10

Exercise 161b

11) The ______________ route is not always the quickest.

12) They could make out the agitated water of the ______ current flowing out to sea.

13) A __________ crystal keeps time accurately by vibrating at a fixed frequency.

14) The pilot could see the ground by looking through _____________ of broken cloud.

15) She wore the ______________ coat that she had to walk in the snow to the shops.

16) Wednesday was the ____________ day: it rained from early morning to evening.

17) Guy Fawkes and his fellow conspirators _____________ the Gunpowder Plot in 1605.

18) She made bandages by ____________ a sheet into long, narrow strips of material.

19) The pair of nesting swans had a __________ of four eggs.

20) The _____________ in her diary ended on 10th September.

Score /10

© 2006 Stephen Curran

Across

161

6. Included in a calculation.
8. The least dry.
10. Emerged from an egg.
11. To grip something firmly.
12. Items included in a list or book.
14. More uninteresting and pitiable.
15. Tearing something with a sudden or rough splitting action.
16. Providing the most protection against cold.
19. The act or process of deducting one number or quantity from another.

Down

1. A rigid metal bar used for towing vehicles.
2. With the highest temperature.
3. Small areas of land used for growing a particular crop.
4. A usually colourless transparent crystalline mineral found in rocks.
5. Illegal copies of, for example, documents or paintings.
7. With, or reflecting, the least light.
9. In some unspecified place.
13. An area of rough water caused by winds or opposing currents.
14. Having the least length or height.
17. Being appropriate to, or the right thing for, somebody or something.
18. Succulent.

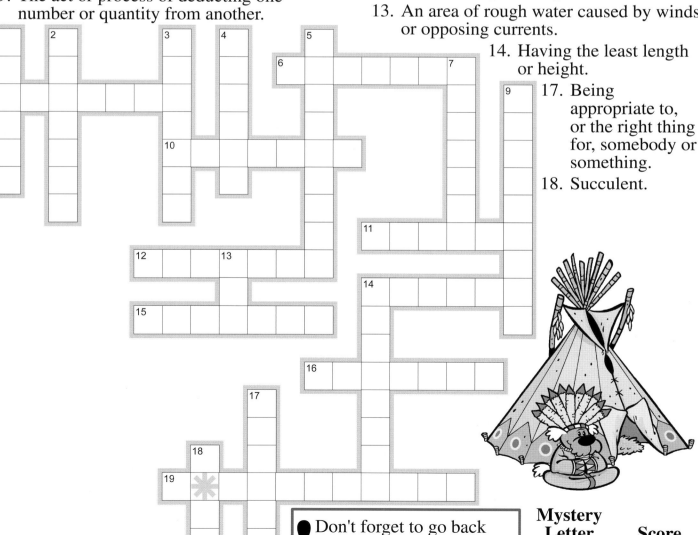

Don't forget to go back to page **37** and complete **Dickens's Mystery Word**.

Mystery Letter

Score

20

Book Seven Word List

accelerate	Briton	counted	eight
accent	buffers	court	electronics
accessory	bulldozer	creature	else
aerobatics	bullet	crept	enamel
aerodrome	buoy	crimson	engage
aeroplane	butcher	cruel	engine
aerosol	calm	cunning	entertain
aim	carrying	cygnet	entries
almighty	catalogue	dairy	except
altimeter	caterpillar	darkest	exchange
ammeter	caught	daughter	excuse
antiques	cellophane	dazzle	factory
appear	centimetre	December	family
archaeology	chasm	deer	farewell
architecture	check	defeat	feather
area	chemistry	delay	fewest
arithmetic	cheque	deliver	figure
astonish	chiropodist	demand	fleet
astronomy	chlorine	depend	flood
athletics	choke	deserve	flour
atrocious	chorister	desire	foe
attack	christen	dictation	foggy
attend	Christianity	different	forgeries
aunt	chromium	dinghy	forgotten
badge	chrysalis	discover	fortune
banana	chrysanthemum	discuss	freedom
barge	circle	disgrace	French
barometer	cities	disgust	fruit
barrel	city	dislike	Germany
basement	claim	distinct	giant
bathe	clamped	distress	gnarled
beginning	clothes	divide	gnashed
behave	clumsy	dizzy	gnome
belief	clutch	drake	gnomon
believe	coach	drown	greedy
beyond	coffee	drowned	grieve
board	coin	drying	groan
boarder	collar	dumb	grotesque
bonnet	colonel	during	group
bowl	combine	duty	guest
bravery	companion	dwelling	guide
breath	company	earnest	guilty
bridge	conscientious	edge	gymnastics
British	continue	efficient	hatched

Book Seven Word List

health	maintenance	pageant	quite
healthy	meant	palace	rails
hedge	measure	parachute	rare
herd	medal	parallel	reason
herring	member	patches	recall
hoard	memory	pavement	reflector
hollow	mental	pencil	refuse
holy	metal	penicillin	relate
honest	metre	pennant	remember
horrid	millimetre	people	remembered
hottest	millionaire	perpendicular	reply
huge	milometer	petrol	restore
idea	mirror	philately	result
illustration	mirth	photography	retire
infectious	mistake	piano	reward
instead	motion	picnic	rip
Ireland	mountaineering	picturesque	ripping
Irish	moustache	piece	rubber
iron	muddy	pleasant	sadder
irreligious	muscular	pleasure	saucer
irresponsible	mysteries	plimsolls	scaffold
irrigation	nation	plus	scamper
irritable	naughty	pneumatic	scampi
jib	navy	poetry	score
journey	niece	pony	scrap
judge	noisy	potato	screen
juicy	nuclear	potatoes	scripture
karate	nuisance	pot-holing	scrooge
khaki	oars	pour	scrounge
kilometre	obey	powder	search
knight	obeyed	praise	season
knit	occupied	prettier	second
knitting	occupy	prettiest	seldom
leather	occur	prize	selfish
level-crossing	ocean	publish	several
life-jacket	October	quads	shilling
literature	office	quarrel	shiver
local	officer	quart	shoe
lodge	orange	quarter	shortest
lollipop	ornithology	quartz	shoulder
losing	ourselves	queer	shrimp
lubricate	overall	question	sign
lunar	overture	quilt	signal
mainsail	owe	quit	signal-box

Book Seven Word List

size	suit	treasure	warn
skill	suiting	tricycle	wealthy
skin-diving	superstitious	trout	wearily
skirt	supplies	truth	weary
slippery	supporter	Tuesday	weather
somewhere	suppose	tunnel	wedding
sour	swamp	tweet	Wednesday
spacious	swap	tweezers	weigh
speedometer	swarm	twig	weight
sprawl	swept	twine	wettest
sprint	swindle	twirl	wharf
squander	swipe	twitter	wharves
square	sword	tyre-lever	whether
squint	tandem	unconscious	whizzed
squirt	taught	unnatural	whom
stampede	thatch	unnecessary	wicked
station	thermometer	unneighbourly	wooden
statue	thread	unnoticed	wore
steadily	throat	using	worry
steer	throne	value	worse
stir	tiger	vase	worship
stirred	tiller	vessel	worst
stoke	toast	viaduct	wound
stout	tomato	vicious	wreck
stretcher	tomatoes	voltmeter	wrong
subtraction	toothbrush	wage	yachting
succumb	towbar	warmest	youth

Congratulations!

You have now learnt to spell **3,220** words, know what they mean and how to use them in a sentence.

Now move on to **Book 8** to learn lots more words to add to your word bank total.

Answers

Exercise 139a
1) bullet
2) barrel
3) dictation
4) distress
5) astonish
6) quarrel
7) rubber
8) distinct
9) company
10) prize

Exercise 139b
11) disgrace
12) companion
13) station
14) size
15) publish
16) discover
17) discuss
18) motion
19) dislike
20) nation

Exercise 140a
1) question
2) combine
3) belief
4) piece
5) forgotten
6) occur
7) quart
8) occupied
9) wharves
10) coffee

Exercise 140b
11) believe
12) hollow
13) grieve
14) quarter
15) ourselves
16) horrid
17) occupy
18) appear
19) wharf
20) niece

Exercise 141a
1) stirred
2) skirt
3) office
4) knitting
5) tomatoes
6) taught
7) bonnet
8) mirror
9) skill
10) daughter

Exercise 141b
11) potatoes
12) caught
13) knight
14) naughty
15) potato
16) knit
17) stir
18) tomato
19) different
20) officer

Crossword No. 139

Crossword No. 140

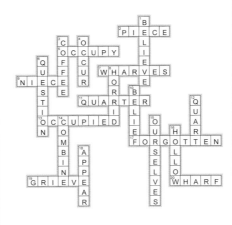

Crossword No. 141

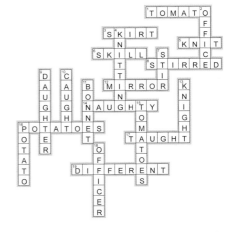

Letter = R

Letter = C

Letter = I

Answers

Exercise 142a
1) cunning
2) *Treasure*
3) muddy
4) shilling
5) continue
6) steadily
7) pleasure
8) tunnel
9) butcher
10) weary

Exercise 142b
11) value
12) thread
13) pleasant
14) poetry
15) Suppose
16) statue
17) wearily
18) foe
19) instead
20) measure

Exercise 143a
1) dwelling
2) youth
3) tiger
4) vessel
5) throat
6) obeyed
7) herring
8) wedding
9) calm
10) swept

Exercise 143b
11) reward
12) wound
13) toast
14) shoe
15) group
16) groan
17) crept
18) coach
19) defeat
20) obey

Exercise 144a
1) leather
2) meant
3) beginning
4) prettier
5) shiver
6) health
7) beyond
8) wealthy
9) recall
10) delay

Exercise 144b
11) prettiest
12) deliver
13) breath
14) weather
15) healthy
16) journey
17) result
18) demand
19) feather
20) depend

Crossword No. 142

Letter = A

Crossword No. 143

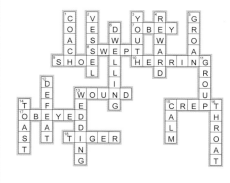

Letter = H

Crossword No. 144

Letter = R

Answers

Exercise 145a
1) aim
2) queer
3) screen
4) deer
5) drown
6) guide
7) warn
8) powder
9) engage
10) drowned

Exercise 145b
11) greedy
12) guest
13) praise
14) dairy
15) guilty
16) claim
17) freedom
18) petrol
19) steer
20) fleet

Exercise 146a
1) medal
2) season
3) Ireland
4) behave
5) British
6) refuse
7) mental
8) bravery
9) retire
10) board

Exercise 146b
11) reason
12) desire
13) iron
14) restore
15) metal
16) Briton
17) Irish
18) relate
19) deserve
20) crimson

Exercise 147a
1) trout
2) Germany
3) bathe
4) hedge
5) stout
6) attend
7) December
8) wreck
9) edge
10) sour

Exercise 147b
11) judge
12) October
13) vase
14) badge
15) flour
16) square
17) herd
18) rare
19) attack
20) wrong

Crossword No. 145
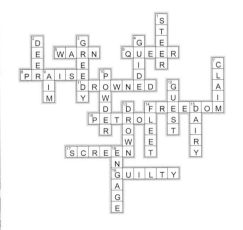

Letter = M

Crossword No. 146
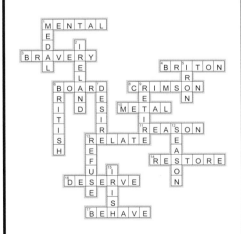

Letter = A

Crossword No. 147
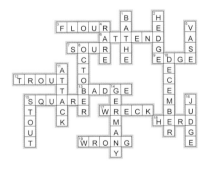

Letter = O

At the Fire Station				
1. DRIVER	2. AXE	3. POLE	4. VISOR	5. FIREMAN
6. LADDER	7. FLAMES	8. HELMET	9. LEGGINGS	10. FIRST AID KIT
11. FIRE ENGINE	12. EXTINGUISHER	13. SIREN	14. HOSE-REEL	15. TELEPHONE

The Train Set				
1. BUFFER	2. ENGINE-SHED	3. TENDER	4. CONTROL BOX	5. LOCOMOTIVE
6. TRUCK	7. TUNNEL	8. BOGEY	9. POINTS	10. SWITCH
11. FOOTBRIDGE	12. SIGNAL	13. CARRIAGE	14. SIGNAL BOX	15. FLAG

Answers

Exercise 148a

1) score
2) check
3) remembered
4) factory
5) lodge
6) suit
7) fruit
8) pavement
9) whether
10) wore

Exercise 148b

11) remember
12) sword
13) Member
14) basement
15) banana
16) whom
17) memory
18) bridge
19) bowl
20) orange

Crossword No. 148

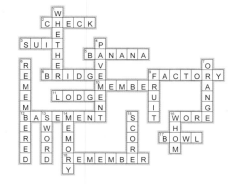

Letter = A

Exercise 149a

1) excuse
2) piano
3) creature
4) eight
5) figure
6) using
7) shoulder
8) scripture
9) exchange
10) weight

Exercise 149b

11) dumb
12) entertain
13) duty
14) pour
15) except
16) weigh
17) during
18) court
19) huge
20) truth

Crossword No. 149

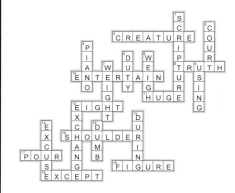

Letter = T

Exercise 150a

1) mistake
2) *Cities*
3) worship
4) reply
5) sign
6) drying
7) giant
8) coin
9) worse
10) engine

Exercise 150b

11) carrying
12) worry
13) noisy
14) signal
15) circle
16) foggy
17) worst
18) divide
19) City
20) Palace

Crossword No. 150

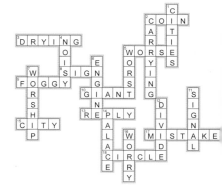

Letter = R

Answers

Exercise 151a
1) family
2) second
3) earnest
4) *Clothes*
5) throne
6) choke
7) area
8) seldom
9) idea
10) wicked

Exercise 151b
11) search
12) several
13) honest
14) people
15) quite
16) French
17) fortune
18) local
19) selfish
20) owe

Exercise 152a
1) disgust
2) clumsy
3) saucer
4) Wednesday
5) navy
6) collar
7) wooden
8) Holy
9) losing
10) Pencil

Exercise 152b
11) Ocean
12) picnic
13) arithmetic
14) cruel
15) Tuesday
16) pony
17) aunt
18) flood
19) farewell
20) else

Exercise 153a
1) catalogue
2) perpendicular
3) gnomon
4) lunar
5) superstitious
6) unnecessary
7) unneighbourly
8) atrocious
9) gnashed
10) gnarled

Exercise 153b
11) muscular
12) vicious
13) unnatural
14) spacious
15) nuclear
16) unnoticed
17) Conscientious
18) unconscious
19) infectious
20) gnome

Crossword No. 151

Letter = O

Crossword No. 152

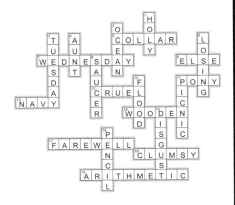

Letter = N

Crossword No. 153

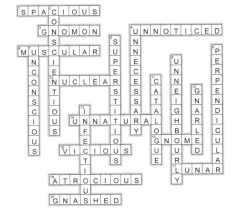

Letter = D

At the Circus
1. SPOTLIGHT
2. FIRE EATER
3. JUGGLER
4. BUMPER
5. RINGMASTER
6. CIRCUS RING
7. CLOWN
8. TRAMPOLINE
9. CATCHER
10. BIG TOP
11. CLUB
12. SOMERSAULT
13. TOP HAT
14. SAFETY NET
15. LEOTARD

On the Village Green
1. FOOTBALL
2. BANDSTAND
3. FIELDER
4. DRUM
5. KITE
6. FOOTPATH
7. DUCK
8. PORCH
9. THATCH
10. POND
11. BENCH
12. LEAD
13. BOWLER
14. WICKET
15. HAMPER

Answers

Exercise 154a

1) illustration
2) aerodrome
3) buoy
4) tiller
5) Caterpillar
6) aerosol
7) literature
8) pennant
9) overall
10) oars

Exercise 154b

11) aeroplane
12) *Overture*
13) lollipop
14) aerobatics
15) mainsail
16) life-jacket
17) dinghy
18) bulldozer
19) jib
20) architecture

Exercise 155a

1) thermometer
2) cellophane
3) chorister
4) chemistry
5) parallel
6) chromium
7) chasm
8) picturesque
9) ammeter
10) cheque

Exercise 155b

11) chrysanthemum
12) Christianity
13) grotesque
14) chlorine
15) chiropodist
16) plimsolls
17) chrysalis
18) millionaire
19) christen
20) penicillin

Exercise 156a

1) buffers
2) millimetre
3) level-crossing
4) signal-box
5) accent
6) altimeter
7) voltmeter
8) viaduct
9) centimetre
10) hoard

Exercise 156b

11) accelerate
12) speedometer
13) boarder
14) rails
15) metre
16) irreligious
17) almighty
18) barometer
19) kilometre
20) accessory

Crossword No. 154

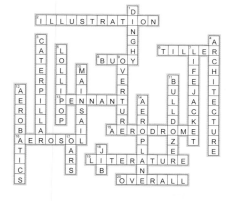

Crossword No. 155

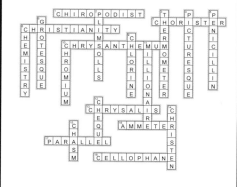

Crossword No. 156

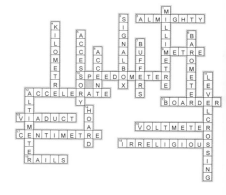

Letter = O

Letter = A

Letter = G

Answers

Exercise 157a
1) ornithology
2) philately
3) tandem
4) photography
5) electronics
6) astronomy
7) skin-diving
8) Archaeology
9) karate
10) pot-holing

Exercise 157b
11) athletics
12) reflector
13) yachting
14) irritable
15) tricycle
16) mountaineering
17) irresponsible
18) antiques
19) gymnastics
20) irrigation

Exercise 158a
1) lubricate
2) tyre-lever
3) moustache
4) efficient
5) pageant
6) parachute
7) khaki
8) squint
9) enamel
10) quilt

Exercise 158b
11) barge
12) squirt
13) milometer
14) pneumatic
15) stampede
16) maintenance
17) quads
18) quit
19) stoke
20) colonel

Exercise 159a
1) cygnet
2) scampi
3) thatch
4) swipe
5) scrounge
6) stretcher
7) swamp
8) shrimp
9) scaffold
10) plus

Exercise 159b
11) clamped
12) twig
13) scamper
14) tweezers
15) dazzle
16) swarm
17) scrooge
18) swap
19) scrap
20) twine

Crossword No. 157
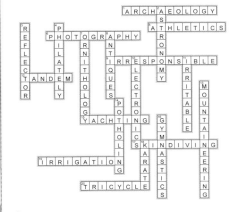

Crossword No. 158
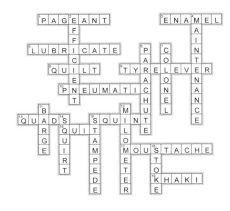

Crossword No. 159
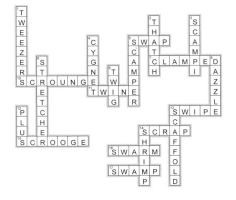

Letter = N

Letter = B

Letter = L

Answers

Exercise 160a

1) sprint
2) supplies
3) drake
4) squander
5) mysteries
6) sprawl
7) fewest
8) succumb
9) wage
10) whizzed

Exercise 160b

11) swindle
12) slippery
13) dizzy
14) tweet
15) mirth
16) twirl
17) nuisance
18) toothbrush
19) twitter
20) supporter

Crossword No. 160

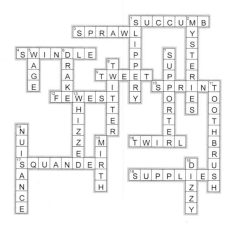

Letter = W

Exercise 161a

1) juicy
2) forgeries
3) somewhere
4) hottest
5) sadder
6) towbar
7) subtraction
8) counted
9) suiting
10) darkest

Exercise 161b

11) shortest
12) rip
13) quartz
14) patches
15) warmest
16) wettest
17) hatched
18) ripping
19) clutch
20) entries

Crossword No. 161

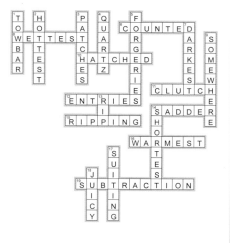

Letter = U

Mystery Word

R C I A H R M A

A R M C H A I R

Mystery Word

O A T R O N D

T O R N A D O

Mystery Word

O A G N B L W U

B U N G A L O W

PROGRESS CHARTS

Scores

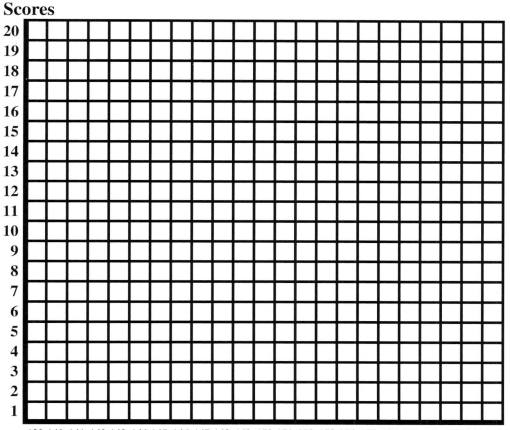

139 140 141 142 143 144 145 146 147 148 149 150 151 152 153 154 155 156 157 158 159 160 161

Exercises

Shade in your score for each exercise on the graph. Add them up for your total score out of 460. Ask an adult to work out the percentage.

Total Score

Percentage

A

Scores

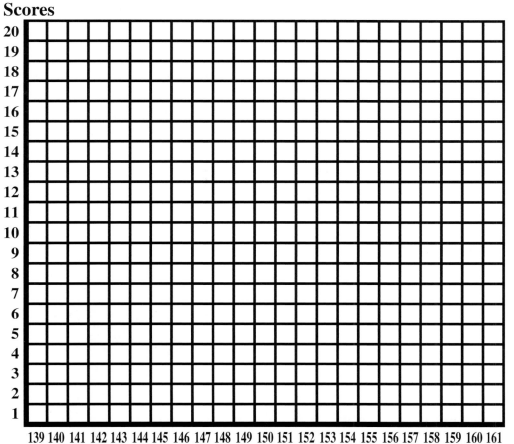

139 140 141 142 143 144 145 146 147 148 149 150 151 152 153 154 155 156 157 158 159 160 161

Crosswords

Shade in your score for each crossword on the graph. Add them up for your total score out of 460.

Total Score

Percentage

B

For the average percentage add %A and %B and divide by 2

Overall Percentage

CERTIFICATE OF

ACHIEVEMENT

This certifies

_____

has successfully completed

Key Stage 2
Spelling & Vocabulary
WORKBOOK **7**

Overall percentage
score achieved

%

Comment _____

_____

Signed _____
(teacher/parent/guardian)

Date _____